The Trying Flapeze

and other puzzle poems

Collected by John Foster

Illustrated by Tony Ross

OXFORD
UNIVERSITY PRESS

OXFORD
UNIVERSITY PRESS

Great Clarendon Street, Oxford OX2 6DP

Oxford University Press is a department of the University of Oxford.
It furthers the University's objective of excellence in research, scholarship,
and education by publishing worldwide in

Oxford   New York

Auckland   Cape Town   Dar es Salaam   Hong Kong   Karachi
Kuala Lumpur   Madrid   Melbourne   Mexico City   Nairobi
New Delhi   Shanghai   Taipei   Toronto

With offices in

Argentina   Austria   Brazil   Chile   Czech Republic   France   Greece
Guatemala   Hungary   Italy   Japan   Poland   Portugal   Singapore
South Korea   Switzerland   Thailand   Turkey   Ukraine   Vietnam

Oxford is a registered trade mark of Oxford University Press
in the UK and in certain other countries

British Library Cataloguing in Publication Data available

ISBN-13: 978-0-19-276314-3
ISBN-10: 0-19-276314-8

3 5 7 9 10 8 6 4 2

Designed by Mike Brain Graphic Design Limited, Oxford

Printed in Great Britain by Cox & Wyman Ltd

Contents

Looking for the Answer?

Ian Bland

Take the letter after L in the UNEXPLAINED!
Then the penultimate letter in PUZZLEMENT!
Find the curliest letter in CURIOSITY!
And the foremost letter in WONDERING!
Find the third vowel in NOSINESS!
And the second consonant in PRYING!

Put them all together and

You've found the . . . ?

The Trying Flapeze

Liz Brownlee

Dear Mad and Dum,
I have pis throblem
with my bead and hottom,
due to sying flomersaults.
I must have mean bad
to leave home, Dum and Mad
for a life in the Tig Bop.
I guess my slittle lip'll
mean I'll trever again do niple
tackflips or bumbles.
My bead looks like a hall,
I'm four inches tess lall
and my jords are all wumbles.
I'm homing come,
Your raving son,
Loymond

Mad and Du

ᴍ ᴠᴠᴠ
ᴍᴠᴠᴠ

Dear Mr and Mrs Spangle,

I enclose a note from your son Raymond, who met with a nasty accident on the flying trapeze last week. I have taken the liberty of also enclosing a translation*. It appears that since the severe blow to his head he mixes up the front letters of some of his words.

Sincerely,

I. M. A. Ringmaster

*see page 54

My Promble

Pam Gidney

I have a promble with my spelling—
The letters are a jumble.
My sorties come back all scorsed out
And all my cheaters grumble.

They think I do it just for nuf,
Or simply to nanoy them.
They won't beelive it's not a joke,
And so they don't jenoy them.

But I can't help it, onesthly,
It's not my flaut at all.
I think my way of spingell
Is most rigonial.

Don't you?

Reflections

Paul Bright

You need a mirror
To admire a verse
In reverse.

And still there's bits
That can't be read
Unless you stand them on their head.

Upside Down Poem

John Foster

The whole
world
seems
to have gone
upside down.
That's why
I've got
this puzzled
frown.

I am
in my
bedroom
bouncing
on my bed.
I am
in my
bedroom
standing
on my head.

Colour Clue Haiku

Daphne Kitching

Anger! Danger! Stop!
Colour of warnings and blood,
Cheerful, glowing blaze.

Prize fish from fairgrounds,
Shiny precious wedding rings,
Kings' crowns and treasure.

Outdoor number one,
Envy and sickness cause this,
Yellow and blue mixed.

Royal, sky, navy,
Feeling sad or unhappy,
Police car's flashing light.

Tongues, toes, pigs (or ham),
Girls are often dressed in this,
Boys *can* wear it too!

Roads, mist, November,
Image of fading dullness,
Lifting black with white.

Cheerfulness and fruit,
Bills of ducks and male blackbirds,
Our favourite juice.

Fluffy hen babies,
Shining gift of the bright sun,
Dusters and grapefruit.

The Lithper'th Thtory

Pam Gidney

Thally Thornton'th thkinny thithter
Had the motht thtupendouth blithter.
Thuthan thought that they thould lanthe it.
Thally thaid, 'I thouldn't chanthe it!'
But Thuthan thouted, with thome thpirit,
'Thut up, Thally! Whothe heel ith it?'
Thally thaid, 'It'th yourth, thank heaventh.
I bet your thoeth are thithe eleventh!'

'Thtop thith noithe!' their mother thaid,
'And thtick thith plathter on inthtead.'

That made the pair of them dethitht!

(I hope *you* haven't got a lithp?)

To Slim or Not to Slim

Richard Edwards

Uncle Slim said to Jim:
'You're too fat. You should slim.'
'Who?' said Jim. 'You,' said Slim. 'Me?' said Jim,
'I'm too fat?' 'Yes,' said Slim.
'I'm not fat,' answered Jim,
'If I slim, I'll be thin, Uncle Slim.'

At that moment Old Jim
Came along. 'Jim,' said Slim,
'Don't you think Jim should slim?' 'What?' said Jim,
'Jim should slim?' 'Yes,' said Slim.
'No,' said Jim, 'not young Jim,
If Jim slims, he'll be slimmer than Slim.'

'Who?' said Slim. 'Slim,' said Jim,
'Not you, Slim, but young Slim.'
'Oh,' said Slim, 'Slim's much slimmer than Jim.'
'Yes,' said Jim. 'Slim's too slim.'
'Who's too slim, Jim?' said Jim.
'Slim's too slim, Jim,' said Jim. 'Yes,' said Slim.

'Here he comes!' cried Old Jim.
'Who?' said Slim. 'Not young Slim?'
'Yes,' said Jim. 'Hallo, Slim.' 'Hallo, Jim.'
'Slim, Slim thinks Jim should slim.'
'No, Jim's slim, aren't you, Jim?'
'Yes, Slim.' 'Yes,' said Slim. 'Jim, Slim, Jim, swim?'

Secret Message

Tim Hopkins

I'm fonder view,
A door ewe,
Were ship ewe,
Add mire ewe;
My art beat sly Kenny thing.

The Valentine Message

Granville Lawson

Dear Christine,
    I know you are clever
    And you can sing too
    So let's get together
    I'd be lost without you!
      Love from Jim

To discover Christine's reply, read the third word of each line.

NIc t Cya!

Brenda Williams

2nIt or 2morO
Bt Lt it B SOn
Lts Gt 2gtha
BI the LIt of the MOn

Fone Fantasy

Alison Chisholm

they only eva use me
2 txt luv notes 2 1 anuva
dnt they reliz
I need 2 b
prt of the actn?
fones have feelings 2

A short tXt poem—2 sAv tIm n munE

George Moore

O DrE me
wotz this I C
wotev nXt
sum vurs in tXt.
thats rElE bad
N slItlE mad.
but then its clEr
sno bad IdEa
U rIt poems lIk thEs
with total Es
U dont Us wurdz
ther 2 absurd
abreV8shun
Ads creAshun.
so wen Ur Tcha
trIs to Bcha
bI Rsking U
4 a vurs or 2
dont get 2 vXt

wrIt them in tXt
B brIt n brEzE
its EzE PzE.
U feel rIt clevr
2 rIm on 4 evr
n wen Miss Gunn
Cs wot Uv dun
shell B Xcited
n kwIt DlIted
she shor wont h8 it
shell aprEC8 it.
Ul get hI mRx
top of the clRs
U just C
RelI on me.

(1 litl thing B4 U do—
dont tell her that I told U
2)

11

I'm Amazed

Alan Hayward

Two O'clock. I'm in the maze at Hampton Court—I really think they flipping ought to change the name to Hampton Caught. Three O'clock. Oh, dear, I'm trapped without a doubt—I'm far inside and can't get out—And no one hears me when I shout. Four O'clock. It's not as easy as it looked—I don't know what to do, I'm hooked—Help! Take me home! My tea is cooked! Rescuer. 'Don't panic, kid, just follow me—You'll still be home in time for tea!'

Maze

Gina Douthwaite

```
          f   leaves   s   is   sky.
A pattern of p       a      h high.
              a      l I   hedges
   Apart      t             h
              h             e
First I through             d
              u             g
              r             e
Privet in front,            s
          left,   privet
          t             t  blimey!
Once caught in          h  e
     a        e         t  h
     n        n right   e  i
tear-away               j  n
                        a  d
          c             w  me
          i   There's   s  a cul-de-sac
          l             o
          d             o
          r   way out. How did I
      I'  e
      m   n ever come back?        get
  R       o
  o   I'  n        T is frightening!
  u   so           h                n
  n                i                ?
  d a confused.    s
  o       r     another,
  r       o
  n       u
wonder then und     discover...
  w       n
  h                 to   daze.
  a                      a
  M   t I'm going        a     in
  o   o                  a
  r   r e hedges!    I'm
  e and get          m
Will I ever  t       a
             o       z
             u     this e
             t     f   ?...
                   o
```

13

The Computer Mouse Tail Trail

Philip Burton

Start in the middle
Follow the marks of each tail (–)
How many lots of C–O–M–P–U–T–E–R–M–O–U–S–E (mice?)
Can you find on this trail?

```
P – U – T – E – R – M – O – U
|                           |
M   R – M – O – U – S – E   S
|   |                   |   |
O   E   E – R – M – O   C   E
|   |   |           |   |
C   T   T   C – O   U   O
|   |   |   |   |   |   |
E   U   U – P – M   S   M
|   |               |   |
S   P – M – O – C – E   P
|                       |
U – O – M – R – E – T – U
```

14

Number Search

John Foster

Find the numbers 1–10

I am the shape of a broken arrow.
I am a netball post with a hoop.
I am a swan upon a river.
I am a ladle for serving soup.
I am a pair of steel handcuffs.
I am a bird upon the wing.
I am a hook on a fishing line.
I am a kite that's lost its string.
I am a matchstick, thin and straight.
I am a knife beside a plate.

Minus the Fun!

Ian Bland

From 50 take away . . .
- The Prime Minister's door!
- The letters in the alphabet!
- The wives of King Henry the VIII!

Now add . . .
- A baker's dozen
- The second highest odd number under 20!
- The eyes on a Cyclops!

Now divide by . . .
- The wise monkeys!

Did you get it?
(Unlucky!)

Teacher's Torture

Mary Green

Add two times twenty-two,
To twelve and twenty more,
Take forty-five from fifty-five,
Add four by forty-four.

Add six and six to sixteen,
To eighteen by eleven,
To nine and nine and ninety-nine,
Add nine from ninety-seven.

Add thirty-three and thirteen,
Take seven from twenty-four,
Add seventy-seven to sixty-six,
And total up your score.

You can count them on your fingers,
You can count them on your toes,
You can count them out with counters,
You can count them out in rows.

And when you've got the answer,
When you're sure, and only then—
You can add another hundred
And count them all again!

17

whatspunctuation

John Foster

whatspunctuationweallneed
itsothatwecanread
whatotherswritewithoutitwed
besoconfusedwewouldnotknow
ifweshouldstoporgo
onreadingwewouldlosetheflow
ofwhatthewritermeanttosay
yeswedallloseourway
sopunctuationsheretostay

Too Wise You Are

Anon.

A rebus is a puzzle in which pictures, letters, numbers, and small diagrams are used to represent syllables and words.

Here is a well-known rebus. Can you solve it?

YY U R

YY U B

I C U R

YY 4 me

Trouble Sleeping?

Richard Caley

👁 1der what 2 do 2day

Jane Clarke

👁 1der what 2 do 2day . . .

👁 'll run away 2 C.

👁 'll join a b🖐 of pir8s.

👁 'd like U 2 come with me.

⊕ need wooden l🐔 and p🌭s,

⊕ need patches for our 👁s.

⊕ scour the Cs for treasure

and wrestle octop👁.

U h8 slimy 10tacles?

U h8 the s👁t of C?

Then ⊕ watch a pir8 movie

And eat 🐟 and chips 4 T.

Re:bus

Mike Johnson

🕐 was getting l8,

had I 4got10 the right d8?

Where on 🌍 were they;

would they 🔙 ⬆️ 2day?

Bgan 2 get fran✔, ✝, and glum,

couldn't (*●*) 2B thought dumb:

no 🦵← –k +d 2 fuss,

they missed the 3→¼ 🚌 !

Which Route?

Richard Caley

From the word wheel shown below
Work out where our man did go
Match the letters, break the code
Find the route our cyclist rode.

UILN SRH SLFHV ZG MFNYVI UREV

_ _ _ _   _ _ _   _ _ _ _ _   _ _   _ _ _ _ _ _   _ _ _ _

ZOLMT GSV OVMTGS LU XSVHGMFG WIREV

_ _ _ _ _   _ _ _   _ _ _ _ _ _   _ _   _ _ _ _ _ _ _ _   _ _ _ _ _

KZHG GSV UZIN LM XSVHGMFG OZMV

_ _ _ _   _ _ _   _ _ _ _   _ _   _ _ _ _ _ _ _ _   _ _ _ _

ILFMW GSV KZIP ZMW YZXP ZTZRM.

_ _ _ _ _   _ _ _   _ _ _ _   _ _ _   _ _ _ _   _ _ _ _ _.

The Lost Pharaoh

Richard Caley

Use the hieroglyphs on show
To find the name of our pharaoh
It may prove quite a tricky quest
But have a go and try your best.

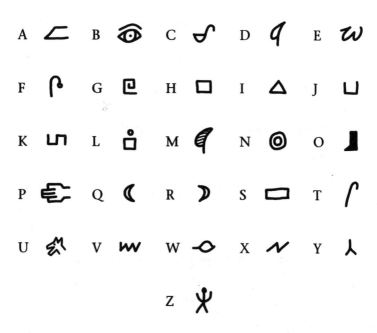

His first is in  but not found in 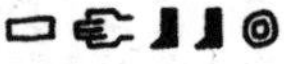 ____

His second in  but never in  ____

His third is in 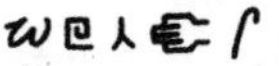 and also in  ____

Whilst his fourth is in 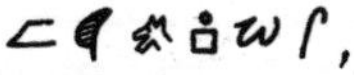, 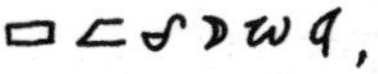,
and  ____

His fifth is in 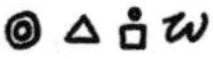 and also in  ____

The next is in  but not found
in  ____

His seventh starts  and also
starts  ____

While his eighth is in  where he
should go ____

His ninth is in  and there appears thrice ____

While his tenth's found in  and there
crops up twice ____

His last is in  and should make it clear ____

The name of the pharaoh who lies hidden here.

Word Square

Bill Longley

Each line is a clue to a four-letter word which goes both across and down at its number to make a 'magic square'.

1. It twinkles high above the moon.
2. This records a favourite tune.
3. Animals—our nearest brothers?
4. This word covers 'all the others'.

	1	2	3	4
1				
2				
3				
4				

Puzzle King

Philip Waddell

Clues

1) What time?
2) A jigsaw perhaps?
3) _ _ and fro
4) _ _ llo (Greeting)
5) Not out
6) F _ _ _ (Tumble)
7) D _ _ _ (Finished)
8) B _ _ _ (Rubber group?)
9) Child _ _ _ _ er (Babysitter)
10) D _ _ (Noise)
11) _ _ ten (Frequently)
12) _ _ _ tory (It's in the past)

13) Go from place to place
14) The top grade
15) _ _ _ t (Strike with the forehead)
16) W _ _ _ (You'll need these about you during tests)
17) The partner of Mrs
18) In which pupils spend most of their school day
19) Begins
20) Where teachers take refuge during breaks

21) _ _ _ _ er (Shrivel)
22) Male monarchs
23) _ _ _ re (Not here)
24) Dis _ _ _ _ _ _ (Became liquid)
25) _ is for apple
26) What a queue does at a bus stop
27) Munches quietly
28) It writes with lead
29) You shouldn't need any more of these!

27

Evil Eye

Louis Fidge

With its evil eye, the whirlwind twists and turns. It spirals and spins, roaring and ranting as it rages around, destroying, smashing, and flattening everything that stands in its way. A trail of devastation and destruction is left in its wake. Like wrecked lives, wrecked homes, wrecked dreams. Like a malevolent force it rears its ugly head and snarls. Where does it come from? Where does it go? Evil evil eye

Witches' Chant

Kate Williams

Find the jewel that ends the chant.

daddylonglegspiderattlesnakelfoxgloveelizardeadly-nightshadeye-of-leopardewdropoisonous-berrieshadowizardiamondgiantoadstooladybirdragonettlestingoblinewtiger'sclawormaggotoad

Staircase Poem

John Foster

This is a staircase poem.
Can you find your way down,
Making very, very
Sure that you see the letter,
Especially placed on each step,
Indicating that you must
Not hurry, but
Take special *care*.

30

Find the Family Secret

Kate Williams

Meet the Gillespies: Steve, Paul, Ian, Emma, and Sarah.
There's something special about these brothers and sisters:
they are all . . . . s.
The missing word is hidden eight times in the lines below,
and twice in the top line above!

The Gillespies love delicious pies,
especially shepherd's pies,
candyfloss pies,
and wispy watercress pies.
But the Gillespies' most scrumptious pies
are good old squashed-flies pies.

Cross Words

Trevor Harvey

If you get cross—and scowl and mutter—
Are THESE among the words you utter . . . ?

Twerp! Swindler!
Nitwit! Dope!
Sadcase! Hate You!
Armpit! Goon!
Rogue! Bogey!
Cats Poo! Twit!
Nitwit! Ogre! *and* Buffoon!

Now place those words in the grid below—
And you'll 'spell out' what children know
Adults shout, whenever you
Say *far more* than you OUGHT to do . . . !

```
            _ _ [_] T

                    [_] _ _ F _ _ _
      _ A _ _ _ _ [_]
                    [_] _ O _

        _ _ G _ [_]
                [_] _ R _
    _ _ _ _    _ O [_]
                [_] _ G _ _

        _ _ _ _ [_]
                [_] _ _ P _ _
    _ _ _ N _ _ _ [_]
                [_] _ _ E
    _ _ _ _    _ _ [_]
                [_] _ _ W _ _
                [ ! ]
```

32

About Me

Bernard Young

I'm in Rome
I'm in Cromer

I'm in chrome
I'm not in aroma

I'm in time
I'm in slime!

I'm in meat
I'm in mime

I'm in measure
I'm in mellow

I'm in melon
I'm not in yellow

I must be famous
I'm in fame

Am I in trouble?
I'm in blame!

I'm in dome
I'm in gnome

Now you've met *me*
I'm going home

Who Are We?

James Carter

I am in Ian
you'll find me in James
(you'll find us in Susan)
—and just me in names

And I am in Tim
but also in him
we're all in Wendy—
who are we?

A Question of Names

John Foster

Why is Pip like Pop
But Bob not like Rob?
Why is Mum like Dad
But Nan not like Gran?

Why is Anna like Hannah
But Eve not like Steve?
Why is Ada like Otto
But Lil not like Jill?

Find Six Palindromes

Eric Finney

Each nonsense poem contains a palindrome consisting of several words. No. 2 also poses another problem!

1. Eve said to a man
   In the Garden of Eden,
   'Your name—is it George or Fred?'
   The young man looked up
   From the plot he was weeding:
   'Madam, I'm Adam,' he said.

2. Find a number that's never odd or even.
   Now there's a teaser for you, Steven!

3. You can step on a carpet
   A rug or a mat
   And there'll be little
   Cause for regrets;
   But just mind the tortoise,
   The dog, and the cat.
   I'm telling you:
   Step on no pets!

4. The fruit bowl is empty
   Of kiwi and kumquat,
   There's no apple,
   No lemons, no melon.
   The question I'm asking is
   Who scoffed the lot?
   Was it Harold
   Or Harriet or Helen?

5. In exile Napoleon sighed, downcast,
   'Able was I ere I saw Elba.
   Still, it's no good brooding on the past:
   Waiter, bring me a large peach Melba.'

6. To settle a quarrel, Herbert and Howard
   Agreed upon pistols at dawn.
   Howard fell dead crying, 'Draw, O coward!'
   Herbert had already drawn.

Alien Nursery Rhyme

Roger Stevens

Can you translate it?

Eye
Did Al? Did Al?
Dick hat on
Dee Fidel
Dick howl jam
Pet offered
immune

Deli dulled hog cleft
Oozy suds fun
Handy cowl Rhonda
Weigh whiff tee
Spoon

A Lipogram

Melissa Lawrence

Mary had a small lamb,
Its coat was ghostly as snow,
And all roads that Mary took
That lamb without doubt would go.

It did tag along with Mary to school,
Although that was a bit of a sin.
How loads of kids did laugh and play,
As a lamb in that classroom was put in.

*Note: A lipogram is a piece of prose or poetry in which one
letter of the alphabet has deliberately not been used. Can you
work out which letter is missing?*

NsrETxtmsging (1)

Brenda Williams

Ths Ltl PGE
Wnt 2 Mrkt
Ths Ltl PGE
Std at HOm

Ths Ltl PGE
At the Mkt
TxtMsgd
The PGE on the FOn

NsrETxtmsging (2)

Brenda Williams

Ltl BO PEp
Hs Lst Hr ShEp
So Cld thm on Hr MObll
She lft thm a txt
To SA She Ws Vxt
& Snt thm Al in2
ExIl

NsrETxtmsging (3)

Brenda Williams

HmpT DmpT
Fl In a POl
Txt hs frnd
To SA its KOl

A Calculated Diet

Damian Harvey

, sit ⬇ my **Grammar** said **2** me

4 we shall have $\frac{45\ +33}{78}$ ✉ **4** R **T**

so I tried an **A** & nibbled on an **E**

But **O** those ✉ tasted *vowel* **2** me

I even **8** a **Z**ed

& rolled $\frac{45\ +33}{78}$ **R**'s around my 👅

But let me tell **U**

Those ✉ tasted **X**

$\frac{45\ +33}{78}$ people like ✉

But 👁'm **A** numbers 🪭

So number crunching

Is my new diet 📋

43

Hidden Chocolate

Pam Gidney

When I take time out
To consider chocolate
It gives me a boost,
Transporting me
To Mars or the Milky Way,
Some galaxy far removed
From everyday life,
Where chocolate oranges grow on trees
And double-deckers don't have wheels.

Me, I'm a drifter, find myself
Twix and between. Can't decide.
I twirl around, like a snowflake
In a passing breeze.
Poetry is no help:
The topic escapes me.
I dream of marble halls,
Wispa of Turkish delight,
Although I do not have a dime
To bless myself with.

I take a picnic,
Rolover in the grass,
An apple covered in toffee
Crisp against my teeth,
And consider
Nature's bounty all around me.
I ignore the snickers
Of passers-by,
The sound of aeroplanes overhead,
And eat my fill,
Then pack my kit, katch
The next bus home.

My Yorkie greets me, barking madly.
We settle down before the fire,
And I unwrap our favourites:
His cubic Munchies,
My Cadbury's Caramel.

(Can you find all 26 of them?)

Who Am I?

John Mole

If A is 1 and B is 2
And so on until Z,
Here's a little puzzle
To work out in your head.

I'm 13 at the kick off
Then 9 then 3 then 8.
Just look at our supporters
Who've crowded through the gate!

1 comes next then 5 and 12
Then straight on to 15.
Just listen to the cheering
Which always greets our team!

Now 23 then back to 5
And 14 to end up with.
Just watch me score a brilliant goal,
The one we win the cup with!

Chirpy, Chirpy, Cheep, Cheep

Mike Elliott

*Do you know your pets? From the clues below find the pets'
names. When you have them all some more are seen in the
MIDDLE going down. See if you can spot the two animals
that are not pets.*

Clues.

1. I hop, nibble, and live in a hutch.
   My fur is very soft to touch.
2. I squeak and I am chased by number 9.
   My long whiskers look just fine.
3. I swim around my watery home.
   I do not ever need a comb.
4. I prowl around both day and night.
   If you saw me you would have a fright.
5. Wheek, wheek I squeal as you go by.
   My bed is straw on which I lie.
6. On my wheel I run and run. I have such a lot of fun.
7. My tiny cubs are very sweet.
   When grown up, YOU they can eat.
8. I can run fast and bark. I love to go in the park.
9. Tom may be my name. Chasing mice is my game.
10. I am like a snake with legs.
    All my babies come from eggs.
11. I am like numbers 6 and 2.
    That should give you a clue.

If you go to the middle, the squares will help you solve
this riddle. From the top, if you search, you can find
these creatures on a perch!

They are _ _ _ _ _ _ _ _ _ _ _ .

1	r						
2	m						
3	g						
4	t						
5	g						
6	g						
7	l						
8	d						
9	c						
10	l						
11	h						

Animalagrams

John Kitching

Does a wasp have paws?
Do apes eat green peas?
Could the plane hold an elephant?
Can you tell me, please?

Could a horse swim ashore?
Could a rat run in tar?
Is a lion on the lino?
Is that going too far?

Would a wolf eat a fowl?
Would it go with the flow?
Does a snail crawl on nails?
I think maybe no.

Shoot a gnu with a gun?
Strip a grizzly bear bare?
Who knows where the newt went?
Did you hear that hare?

Who would mar my poor poem—
—A wee ewe or a ram?
Fourteen animals here,
Each with neat anagram.

Anagram-antics

Pie Corbett

1. Night.
The *tab* flies at night,
the *low* bird glides.
Be *silent*—to hear
Their flight.

2. Fruit.
This *lump* is no bruise
But a purple fruit.
It is *ample*—
the tree that yields syrup.
Lemons are the serious mask.
Pears sound tasty
But are sharp tipped.

3. Poor Mabel!
Some say it makes you *groan*
—others enjoy each note.

Watch out for that *part*—
you could fall in!

Poor *Mabel*—
always responsible
for mistakes.

Tractor

John Rice

An example of 'boustrophedon' or 'ox-writing' where both the lines and the words are reversed. This poem seeks to emulate the up-and-down-the-field ploughing action of the tractor.

Dressed in a coat of mud
lios htiw derettalps dna
the farm tractor coughs and rasps
.taorht dab a htiw nroh yrotcaf a ekil

Huge tyres heave
dleif yggos eht hguorht hguolp eht
churning the dark earth into
.sevaw nezorf ekil sepahs
Seagulls swoop and glide behind
eerf gniwolf snobbir dliw ekil
in some great wind.

Up and down
—gnol yad lla yellav eht pu dna nwod
the tractor never tires.
ecreip sthgil sti gnineve yB
the gathering dusk
sdleif eht revo sllor lworg sti dna
like a tumbling echo.
thgin dellif-rats eht ,ylwolS
covers the countryside in a warm dark
.hguolP tnelis nwo sti sgnirb taht

Postcard Puzzle

Clare Bevan

Hello, Mum—Guess where we are!
We didn't come by bus or car,
We sailed a scruffy sort of ship
That skimmed the land and
    swayed the hip
To walls of wonder, high and steep,
To dusty tunnels hushed with sleep,
To one great beast who gazes down
With ancient eyes and stony frown
At sunlit sands, but no blue sea . . .
ot it? Love from Tut and Me.

Mum

Where's My Holiday?

Granville Lawson

To find the answer take the first letter of the first line, the second letter of the second line and so on.

This place is warm and by the sea
I hope that you will come with me
A very sunny holiday
The charming villa where we'll stay
Is close to beaches safe and clean
The best sand you have ever seen
You must remember suntan oil
While travelling on foreign soil
It's not Madeira, France, or Crete
A plane is ready, take your seat
Beyond the clouds we'll swiftly fly
Wave your arms and say goodbye
Such a lovely holiday
But where's the place, now can you say?

Message on the Table

David Kitchen

Your dinner is in the
Oven because I'm taking
Uncle
Jack
Up to your grandmother's.
She hasn't seen him in years.
There's also extra sauce in
A pan on the stove. It needs
To be warmed through
Even if you manage to get in on time.
Wash up and
Open a can of something if you're still
Really hungry, although you
May not be if you work out my
Secret.

Answers to Puzzles

Page 2: Dear Mum and Dad
I have this problem with my head and bottom due to flying somersaults.
I must have been mad to leave home, Mum and Dad, for a life in the Big To
I guess my little slip'll mean I'll never again do triple backflips or tumbles.
My head looks like a ball, I'm four inches less tall, and my words are all
jumbles. I'm coming home.
Your loving son,
Raymond

Page 4: Reflections— You need a mirror
To admire a verse
In reverse.

And still there's bits
That can't be read
Unless you stand them on their head.

Page 6: Colour Clue Haiku—red, gold, green, blue, pink, grey, orange, yellow.

Page 10: NIc t Cya!— Nice to See You!

Tonight or tomorrow
But let it be soon
Let's get together
By the light of the moon

Page 13: Maze —A pattern of paths through hedges high.
Apart from leaves all I see is sky.
First I turn left, then right, then blimey!
Privet in front, privet behind me.
Once caught in the jaws of a cul-de-sac
can tear-away children ever come back?
There's no way out.   How did I get in?
I'm so confused.   This is frightening!
Round a corner then round another,
wonder what I'm going to discover . . .
More and more hedges!   I'm in a daze.
Will I ever get out of this maze? . . .

Page 15: Number Search—7, 9, 2, 6, 8, 3, 5, 4, 1, 10

Page 16: Minus the Fun!—13

Page 17: Teacher's Torture—999

Page 19: Too wise you are Too wise you be.
I see you are Too wise for me.

Page 20: Trouble Sleeping?—
If at night you cannot sleep,
Then go ahead and count some sheep.

Page 22: Re:bus— Time was getting late,
had I forgotten the right date?
Where on Earth were they:
would they turn up today?
Began to get frantic, cross, and glum,
couldn't bear to be thought dumb:
no need to fuss,
they missed the quarter past three bus!

Page 23: Which Route?—From his house at number five,
Along the length of Chestnut Drive
Past the farm on Windmill Lane
Round the park and back again.

Page 24: The Lost Pharaoh—Tutankhamun

Page 26: Word Square—star, tape, apes, rest

Page 27: Puzzle King. If you completed this puzzle—Congratulations! You did better than Mr King!

W	H	E	N	M	R	K	I	N	G	'	S	M	I	N	D	S	T	A	R	T	S	T	O	W	A	N	D	E	R
I	N	C	L	A	S	S	A	N	D	H	I	S	P	E	N	C	I	L	H	E	C	H	E	W	S
A	P	U	Z	Z	L	E	A	W	A	I	T	S	I	N	T	H	E	S	T	A	F	F	R	O	O	M
W	I	T	H	A	L	L	S	O	L	V	E	D	B	U	T	O	N	E	O	F	I	T	S	C	L	U	E	S

Page 32: Cross Words—I beg your pardon!

Page 40: (1)
NsrETxtmsging
This little piggy
Went to market
This little piggy
Stayed at home

This little piggy
At the market
Text messaged
The piggy on the phone.

Page 41: (2)
Little Bo-Peep
Has lost her sheep
So called them on her mobile
She left them a text
To say she was vexed
And sent them all into
Exile

Page 42: (3)
Humpty Dumpty
Fell in a pool
Text his friend
To say 'It's cool!'

Page 44: Hidden Chocolate. Answers: Time Out, Boost, Mars, Milky Way, Galaxy, Chocolate Oranges, Double Decker, Drifter, Twix, Twirl, Snowflake, Topic, Wispa, Turkish Delight, Marble, Dime, Picnic, Rolo, Toffee Crisp, Bounty, Snickers, Aero, Kit Kat, Yorkie, Munchies, Cadbury's Caramel.

Page 45: Who Am I?—Michael Owen

Page 46: Chirpy, Chirpy, Cheep, Cheep—budgerigars

Page 51: Postcard Puzzle—the Pyramids

Page 52: Where's My Holiday?—the Costa del Sol

Acknowledgements

We are grateful for permission to reproduce the following poems:
Gina Douthwaite: 'Maze', from *Picture a Poem* (Hutchinson 1994), copyright ©
Gina Douthwaite, reprinted by permission of The Random House Group
Limited and Andrew Mann Ltd. **Richard Edwards**: 'To Slim or Not to Slim',
from *The Word Party* (Lutterworth Press 1986), copyright © Richard Edwards,
reprinted by permission of the author. **Louis Fidge**: 'Evil Eye', from *Teaching
Poetry Book 3* (Letts Educational 2002), copyright © Louis Fidge, reprinted by
permission of the author. **Pam Gidney**: 'The Lithper'th Thtory', from *Tongue
Twisters and Tonsil Twizzlers* (Macmillan 1997), copyright © Pam Gidney,
reprinted by permission of the author. **Mary Green**: 'Teacher's Torture', from
The Works 2 (Macmillan 2002), copyright © Mary Green, reprinted by
permission of the author. **Alan Hayward**: 'I'm Amazed', from *Fun Poems*
(Summersdale 1997), copyright © Alan Hayward, reprinted by permission of
the author.

All other poems are published for the first time in this collection by permission
of their authors.
Clare Bevan: 'Postcard Puzzle', copyright © Clare Bevan 2003. **Ian Bland**:
'Looking For the Answer', and 'Minus the Fun!', both copyright © Ian Bland
2003. **Paul Bright**: 'Reflections', copyright © Paul Bright 2003. **Liz Brownlee**:
'Trying Flapeze', copyright © Liz Brownlee 2003. **Philip Burton**: 'The
Computer Mouse Tail Trail', copyright © Philip Burton 2003. **Richard Caley**:
'Trouble Sleeping', 'Which Route?', and 'The Lost Pharaoh', all copyright ©
Richard Caley 2003. **James Carter**: 'Who Are We?', copyright © James Carter
2003. **Alison Chisholm**: 'Fone Fantasy', copyright © Alison Chisholm 2003.
Jane Clarke: 'Eye 1der what 2 to do 2day', copyright © Jane Clarke 2003.
Pie Corbett: 'Anagram-antics', copyright © Pie Corbett 2003. **Mike Elliott**:
'Chirpy, Chirpy, Cheep, Cheep', copyright © Mike Elliott 2003. **Eric Finney**:
'Find Six Palindromes', copyright © Eric Finney 2003. **John Foster**: 'Upside
Down Poem', 'Number Search', 'A Question of Names', 'Staircase Poem', and
'whatspunctuation', all copyright © John Foster 2003. **Pam Gidney**: 'My
Promble', and 'Hidden Chocolate', both copyright © Pam Gidney 2003.
Damian Harvey: 'A Calculated Diet', copyright © Damian Harvey 2003.
Trevor Harvey: 'Cross Words', copyright © Trevor Harvey 2003. **Tim Hopkins**:
'Secret Message', copyright © Tim Hopkins 2003. **Mike Johnson**: 'Re:Bus',
copyright © Mike Johnson 2003. **David Kitchen**: 'Message on the Table',
copyright © David Kitchen 2003. **Daphne Kitching**: 'Colour Clue Haiku',
copyright © Daphne Kitching 2003. **John Kitching**: 'Animalagrams', copyright
© John Kitching 2003. **Melissa Lawrence**: 'A Lipogram', copyright © Melissa
Lawrence 2003. **Granville Lawson**: 'The Valentine Message', and 'Where's My
Holiday?', both copyright © Granville Lawson 2003. **Bill Longley**: 'Word
Square' copyright © Bill Longley 2003. **John Mole**: 'Who Am I?', copyright ©
John Mole 2003. **George Moore**: 'A short tXt poem – 2 sav tim n munE',
copyright © George Moore 2003. **John Rice**: 'Tractor', copyright © John Rice
2003. **Roger Stevens**: 'Alien Nursery Rhyme', copyright © Roger Stevens 2003.
Philip Waddell: 'Puzzle King', copyright © Philip Waddell 2003. **Kate
Williams**: 'Witches' Chant', and 'Find the Family Secret', both copyright ©
Kate Williams 2003. **Brenda Williams**: 'Nic t Cya!', and 'NsrE Txtmsging', all
copyright © Brenda Williams 2003. **Bernard Young**: 'About Me', copyright ©
Bernard Young 2003.